Italian Lambr
Bianca

50 Easy And Quick Dinners For One

50 Delicious one person recipes that take less than 30 minutes to cook.

Life Beauty

ISBN: 9798555345431

Welcome!

30 Easy And Healthy Recipes For Lunch And Dinner

1. Smoky bacon pot noodle for one

Ingredients

1 rasher smoked back bacon, trimmed and chopped

2 spring onions, white and green separated and finely sliced

50g frozen pea quarter tsp paprika

2 tsp cornflour

200ml vegetable stock

150g block straight-to-wok wheat noodle, or equivalent of dried, cooked splash Worcestershire sauce

Method

In a small non-stick pan, fry the bacon for a few mins, add the white parts of the spring onions, peas and paprika, then cook for 1 min more.

Mix the cornflour with a little of the stock to get a paste, then stir this into the pan with the rest of the stock, noodles and a good splash of Worcestershire sauce.

Simmer for a couple of mins until thick and saucy, then scatter with the green parts of spring onion

2. Super steak with bearnaise

Ingredients

2 tbsp vegetable oil

1 medium potato

Potato, peeled and cut into small chunks

200g sirloin steak, preferably Scottish

1 tbsp red wine vinegar

2 tbsp crème fraîche

1 tbsp wholegrain mustard

1 tbsp chopped fresh tarragon

Tarragon green salad, to serve

Method

Heat 1 tablespoon of the oil in a small nonstick frying pan that has a lid. Tip the potatoes into the pan, cover and cook for 10 minutes, shaking the pan occasionally so the potatoes get tossed around. Remove the lid and fry the potatoes uncovered for another 4-5 minutes, until crisp and golden.

Season the steak. About 5 minutes before the potatoes are ready, heat the remaining oil in a small heavy-based frying pan and fry the steak for 1 1/2-2 minutes on each side, depending how you like it done.

Take the steak out of the pan and put it on a warmed plate. Turn down the heat, spoon in the vinegar (it will evaporate immediately), then quickly stir in the crème fraîche and mustard and heat just until they melt and make a sauce. Sprinkle in most of the tarragon, stir and taste for seasoning.

Pour the sauce over the steak and scatter with the remaining tarragon. Serve with the crisp potatoes and a green salad, pour yourself a glass of red wine - and tuck in.

3. Flat chicken with tomatoes, olives and capers

Ingredients

1 boneless, skinless chicken breast a little seasoned flour, for dusting

1 tbsp olive oil, 1 large ripe tomato, chopped

2 tsp capers handful olives splash white wine (or water, if you prefer) chopped chives or parsley

Method

Split the chicken breast almost in half and open it out like a book. Bash with a rolling pin to flatten, then lightly coat in the seasoned flour.

Heat the oil in a pan, add the chicken and cook for 3-4 mins on each side until crisp, browned and cooked through. Remove from the pan and keep warm.

Add the tomato, capers, olives and wine to the pan, season to taste, then bring to the boil. Bubble the sauce for 2-3 mins until the tomatoes are starting to break down, then spoon over the chicken and scatter with chopped herbs.

Delicious with steamed potatoes.

4. Summer risotto for one

Ingredients

450ml vegetable stock, made with half a stock cube

4 asparagus spears, trimmed (trimmings kept) and each spear sliced into 4

200-250g/8-9oz peas in the pod, about 85g/3oz podded (pods kept)

2 tbsp olive oil

1 small onion, finely chopped

85ml risotto rice

3 tbsp white wine (keep the rest of the bottle chilling) small handful of freshly grated parmesan (or vegetarian alternative) small handful of rocket and a few parmesan (or vegetarian alternative) shavings, to serve

Method

Simmer the stock for 10 minutes with the asparagus trimmings and pea pods; these will intensify the flavour. Strain into a jug.

Heat 1 tbsp of the oil in a shallow pan. Add the onion and fry for 5-6 minutes, stirring, until it is soft but not coloured. Add the rice and continue to stir and cook for 1-2 minutes until the grains become see-through at the edges and begin to make 'clicking' noises.

Add the wine (it should bubble and evaporate), then 50ml of the stock. Stir well and simmer gently until all the liquid has been absorbed. Now pour in another 50ml/2fl oz stock and stir again.

Continue adding stock and stir. After about 7 minutes, when half the stock has been added, swirl in the asparagus and peas. Carry on adding stock in small amounts until it has been absorbed; this will take about 10 more minutes. Now the risotto should be a little wet and sloppy and the rice tender with a nutty bite.

Turn off the heat, then gently stir in the grated Parmesan, taste and season. You may need only a little black pepper as the Parmesan and stock are both salty. Spoon the risotto onto a plate, top with the rocket, drizzle with the remaining olive oil and scatter with Parmesan shavings.

5. Fish with peas and lettuce

Ingredients

1 Little Gem lettuce, shredded

2 spring onions, thickly sliced handful frozen peas

1 tbsp olive oil

140g boneless white fish fillet

1 tbsp reduced-fat crème fraîche

Method

Mix together the lettuce, spring onions and peas in a microwave-proof dish. Drizzle with olive oil. Sit fish fillet on top, spoon over crème fraîche, then season. Cover with cling film, then pierce film.

Microwave on Medium for 6-8 mins until the fish is cooked. Lift fish off the lettuce, then give lettuce and peas a good stir. Spoon lettuce mix and sauce onto a plate, then sit fish on top.

6. Anytime eggs

Ingredients

1 tbsp olive oil

2-3 cooked potatoes, sliced handful cherry tomatoes, sliced

2 spring onions, sliced

1 egg, few basil leaves

Method

Heat the oil in a frying pan, then add the potato slices and fry on both sides until brown. Add the tomatoes and spring onions and fry for about 1 min until softened. Season with salt and pepper, then make a space in the pan. Gently break the egg into the space and fry until cooked to your liking. Scatter over the basil leaves and serve.

7. Microwave macaroni and cheese in a mug
Ingredients:

⅓ cup (28g) pasta

¾ cup (175ml) water, cold

4 tablespoons milk

¼ teaspoons cornstarch

4 tablespoons cheddar cheese, grated salt and pepper

Instructions

In a large microwavable mug or large bowl add in the macaroni and the water. You need a large mug as the water will boil up.

Microwave for roughly 3 ½ minutes. You want the pasta to be fully cooked. (timeing is based on my 1200W microwave so your timing might vary)

Pour off the remaining cooking water.

Stir in the milk, cornstarch and shredded cheese and microwave for a final 60 seconds to create your sauce. Stir well, season with salt and pepper and enjoy.

8. 5-Minute vegetarian burrito bowl

Ingredients

1 cup cooked brown rice

1/2 cup black beans, drained and rinsed

2-3 tablespoons salsa, or to taste

1 tablespoon plain Greek yogurt

1 tablespoon shredded cheddar or Mexican-blend cheese

Toppings:

Diced avocado, diced tomato, guacamole, pico de gallo, etc.

Instructions

Prepare brown rice according to package instructions.

In a microwave-safe bowl, combine rice, black beans, salsa, plain Greek yogurt, and shredded cheese.

Microwave on high for 30-60 seconds, or until heated through.

Top with diced avocado, diced tomato, guacamole, pico de gallo, or other desired toppings.

9. Salmon rarebit

Ingredients

Slice granary bread (or a bread of your choice)

½ x 212g can Wild Alaskan Pacific salmon, drained and flaked 1-2 spring onions, thinly sliced

2 tbsp cottage cheese

1 tsp grated horseradish

Horseradish root on a wooden chopping board (optional) 1 tbsp coarsely grated Red Leicester cheese

40g watercress and spinach salad, to serve

Method

Heat grill to high. Toast the bread lightly on both sides.

Mix the salmon and spring onions together and season with pepper only. Spread onto the bread. Mix together the cottage cheese, horseradish (if using) and cheese. Spoon on top of the salmon.

Grill on a high shelf for 1 min, then lower the shelf and continue to grill for a further 3-4 mins or until the topping starts to brown. Serve straight away with a watercress and spinach salad.

10. Tomato and basil omelette

Ingredients

1 ripe tomato

1 tbsp grated vegetarian cheddar

3 basil leaves

1 spring onion, finely chopped

1 tbsp olive oil

2 eggs, beaten

Method

Finely chop the tomato and tip into a bowl with the cheese, basil leaves, spring onion, half the olive oil and some salt and pepper.

Heat the remaining oil in a small, non-stick frying pan, then swirl in the eggs. Cook until done to your liking, then spoon the tomato mix over half of the omelette. Fold omelette over the tomato, leave for about 30 secs, then slide onto a plate. Serve with a salad.

11. Pasta for one

Ingredients

Salt, Dried pasta, Butter, Grated Parmesan

Black pepper

Instructions

Bring a few inches of water, and a generous pinch of salt, to a boil in a saucepan.

Once the water is boiling, grab a handful of long noodles about the diameter of a quarter (about 1-inch) and add it to the pot. Cook the pasta until it is flexible, but not all the way to al dente.

Place a 10" saute pan on the stove next to the pot of pasta and set the burner to medium. Add two pats of butter (2 tablespoons) and use a pasta fork to transfer the pasta to the saute pan.

Pour enough of the pasta cooking water into the saute pan to come about halfway up the noodles (about 1/4 cup). Add a generous pinch of salt and cook the pasta, tossing occasionally, until al dente (or to your liking).

Turn off the heat and toss with enough grated cheese to absorb the remaining liquid in the pan and form a creamy sauce.

Grind plenty of black pepper onto the top of the pasta.

Taste and add more salt if needed. Transfer to a plate, garnish with more cheese, and enjoy!

12. Leek and sage risotto with bacon
Ingredients

1 tbsp olive oil

2 leeks, sliced

4 sage leaves, shredded, or pinch dried

85g risotto rice

Small glass white wine

200ml hot vegetable stock

2-3 rashers streaky bacon

3 tbsp grated parmesan

Parmesan

Method

Heat the oil in a pan, add the leeks and sage and fry for 2 mins until the leeks are starting to soften. Stir in the rice and cook for 1 min, stirring. Add the wine and stock and bring to the boil. Reduce the heat, cover and simmer for 10-12 mins until the rice is tender.

Meanwhile, grill the bacon until golden and crisp. Remove the rice from the heat, then stir in 2 tbsp of the Parmesan and freshly ground pepper. Spoon onto a plate, sprinkle with the remaining Parmesan and top with the bacon.

13. Prawn and coconut laksa

Ingredients

2 tsp oil

1 garlic clove, crushed

1 spring onion, finely chopped

2 tsp finely chopped fresh root ginger

1 green chilli, deseeded and finely chopped juice from ½ lime

100g raw prawns, any size

165ml can coconut milk

Coconut milk in a glass, with half a coconut

100ml chicken or vegetable stock

100g dried egg noodles, chopped coriander, to serve

Method

Heat the oil in a large pan or wok. When hot, throw in the garlic, spring onion, ginger and green chilli. Cook on a medium heat for 3-4 mins, then squeeze in your lime juice.

Stir in the prawns, then add in the coconut milk and stock. Simmer gently for 5 mins on a low heat until the prawns are pink.

Meanwhile, cook your egg noodles in a pan of boiling water for 4 mins until soft. Drain, then tip into the laksa pan. Season to taste, then serve in a bowl, topped with coriander.

14. One person chicken Margherita

Ingredients

1/2 tablespoon olive oil, divided

1 6-ounce boneless, skinless chicken breast
2 tablespoons pesto
1/2 cup halved grape tomatoes

1 ounce shredded mozzarella cheese

For The Lemon Garlic Sauce

1 tablespoons butter

1 clove garlic minced

1/2 teaspoon lemon juice

1 tablespoon chopped parsley

Instructions

Heat oven to 425 degrees F (220 degrees C).

Pour 1/4 tablespoon of the olive oil into the baking dish. Swirl so that the oil coats the bottom of the dish. Place the chicken breast in the baking dish.

Spoon pesto over the chicken breast. Scatter tomatoes around the chicken and drizzle the remaining olive oil over the chicken and the tomatoes.

Bake for 30 minutes.

After the chicken is cooked through, sprinkle Mozzarella cheese over the top. Place the baking dish back into the oven and bake for an additional 5 minutes, until cheese has melted.

Lemon Garlic Sauce

Melt the butter over medium heat in an 8-inch skillet. Add the minced garlic and cook, stirring for 1 minute. Stir in the lemon juice and parsley and cook for a minute. Pour sauce over chicken and enjoy hot.

15. Braised chicken and red potatoes in tarragon broth

Ingredients

1-2 teaspoons of olive oil

1/3 cup finely chopped shallots

1 pound boneless and skinless chicken breast, cut into bite-size pieces

2 ½ cups fat-free chicken broth ½ cup of white wine

1/2 teaspoon fresh tarragon, chopped

1/4 teaspoon black pepper, freshly ground

1 pack red potato wedges, cut into bite-size pieces
2 tablespoons fresh parsley, chopped Diretions

Method

In a large saucepan, heat oil over medium-high heat. Add shallots; sauté for a minute. Put in chicken and continue sautéing for another 2 minutes.

Add the broth, wine, tarragon, salt, and pepper; once boiling simmer for 5 minutes while occasionally stirring. Add the potatoes; simmer until potatoes are tender.

Remove from heat; stir in parsley and serve.

16. Mushroom and Navy-bean stew

Ingredients

1 1/2 tablespoon olive oil

1 medium onion, chopped

4 red potatoes, cut into bite-size pieces

1 pound mushrooms, trimmed and quartered

1/4 teaspoon dried thyme

1-2 tablespoons tomato paste

2 cups water

10 ounces baby spinach leaves

1 can (14 1/2 ounces) navy beans, drained and rinsed

1-2 tablespoons wine vinegar

Ground pepper

Salt

Method

In a Dutch oven or large nonstick skillet, heat oil over medium heat; gently swirl to coat pan.

Add onion and potatoes and sauté until onion is lightly browned, around 10 minutes.

Add the mushrooms, thyme, and salt; cook until mushrooms are tender, around 8 to 10 minutes. Stir in tomato paste and water; cover with lid and cook until potatoes are tender.

Add spinach and beans; cook until heated through. Stir in wine vinegar then season with salt and pepper.

17. Trout with garden salad

Ingredients

1 lemon, a small bunch of dill, half chopped, half left as sprigs

1 rainbow trout, gutted and washed, weighing about 350g

2 tbsp olive oil, plus a little extra for greasing

2 tbsp Greek yogurt

½ garlic clove

4 runner beans, stringed and thinly sliced diagonally

3 radishes, sliced into thin rounds

Method

Preheat the oven to 200C. Slice half the lemon and stuff the slices, with the sprigs of dill, into the cavity of the trout. Lay the fish on an oiled baking sheet and make 4 diagonal slashes on one side about 4 cm long. Drizzle 1 tbsp of olive oil over the fish, season liberally and bake for 15 minutes.

Put the kettle on to boil, then stir the chopped dill into the yogurt with a squeeze of lemon and some salt and pepper, and set aside. Sprinkle salt on the cut side of the garlic clove and rub it on the inside of a small bowl – this is a good way of getting garlic flavour into food without it being too strong.

Empty the boiling water from the kettle into a small saucepan, bring to the boil and cook the runner beans for 3-4 minutes until cooked but still slightly crunchy. Drain the beans and toss them in the garlicky bowl with the radishes and remaining oil.

Serve the fish with the warm beans and the yogurt sauce. Trim the remaining lemon into a wedge to squeeze over the trout and the salad

18. Lemony tuna pita pockets

Ingredients

1 head Baby Gem lettuce

Cucumber

Fresh mint

1 tbsp fresh lemon juice

100g can tuna in brine

2 mini pitta breads

Method

Shred the lettuce and mix with some chopped cucumber, a pinch chopped fresh mint and the lemon juice. Drain and flake the tuna, stir into the salad. Season if you want to. Slit open the pitta-breads and warm briefly in a toaster. Stuff pita pockets with the salad and tuna mix.

19. Chilli cheese omelette

Ingredients

1 spring onion

A few sprigs of fresh coriander

2 large eggs

1 tbsp sunflower oil

½ -1 tsp chopped fresh red chilli, or a
generous pinch dried chilli flakes 25g
mild grated cheddar

Method

Chop the spring onion and coriander quite finely and beat the
eggs together with salt and pepper. Heat the oil in a small
frying pan then tip in the onion, coriander and chilli and stir
round the pan for a second or two so they soften a little. Pour
in the eggs and keep them moving until two thirds have
scrambled.

Settle the eggs back down on the base of the pan, scatter
over the cheese and cook for about a minute until the
omelette is just set and the cheese has melted.

Carefully fold the omelette using a palette knife and slide from
the pan to a serving plate. Eat while the omelette is hot and the
cheese still melted.

20. Vegetarian club sandwich

Ingredients

3 slices granary bread

1 large handful watercress

1 carrot, peeled and coarsely grated

Small squeeze lemon juice

1 tbsp olive oil

2 dessert spoons reduced-fat hummus in a pot

2 tomatoes, thickly sliced

Method

Toast the bread. Meanwhile, mix the watercress, carrot, lemon juice and olive oil together. In a small bowl spread the hummus over each slice of toast. Top 1 slice with the watercress and carrot salad, sandwich with another slice of toast and top with the tomato.

Lay the final slice of bread, hummus side down, then press down and eat as is or cut the sandwich into quarters.

21. Rocket, carrot and ham salad

Ingredients

1 large carrot

2 tbsp fresh orange juice

2 good handful of rocket

2 tbsp pumpkin seed

3-4 wafer thin slices lean ham

Black pepper

Method

Coarsely grate the carrot and mix with the orange juice and some salt, if you want. Mix the rocket with the pumpkin seeds. Top with lean ham and grind over some fresh black pepper.

22. Croque madame with spinach salad
Ingredients

1 thick slice crusty white bread

1½ tsp wholegrain or Dijon mustard

2 thin slices ham, trimmed of fat

50g mature cheddar or other melting cheese, grated

½ tsp cider ò white wine

Vinegà 1 tsp mild olive oil

Oliveoil, plus a little for frying

1egg

Handful baby-leaf spinach from 100g bag few cornichons (optional)

Method

Heat grill to high and lightly toast the bread on both sides. Spread 1 tsp mustard over one side, then top with the ham and cheese. Whisk the remaining mustard and vinegar with 1 tsp oil and seasoning.

Grill the croque for 3 mins, or until the cheese is bubbling and turning golden. Meanwhile, heat a non-stick frying pan. Add a little oil, then crack in the egg and gently fry to your liking. When cooked, lift it on top of the toast. Toss the dressing with the spinach, and cornichons if using, then eat straight away.

23. Smoked salmon layer
Ingredients

½ carrot, peeled

2 radishes, trimmed

Small chunk cucumber

3 tbsp full fat soft cheese

Juice ½ lemon or lime

Small handful coriander leaves, roughly chopped

2 slices smoked salmon

Drizzle of olive oil

Oolive oil, to serve (optional)

Bread and butter, to serve

Method

Grate the carrot, radishes and cucumber, discarding the cucumber seeds. Mix in the cheese, lemon or lime juice and most of the coriander, then season. Lay a slice of salmon on a plate, top with veg mix, then drape over the other slice. Scatter with remaining coriander, drizzle with olive oil and serve with bread and butter.

24. Scrambled omelette toast topper
Ingredients

2 eggs

1 tbsp crème fraîche

25 g cheddar, grated

Small bunch chive, snipped

1 spring onion, sliced

1 tsp oil

3-4 cherry tomatoes, halved

2 slices crusty bread, toasted

Method

Beat together eggs, crème fraîche, cheese and chives with a little seasoning. Heat oil in a pan, then soften spring onion for a few mins. Add tomatoes and warm through, then pour in egg mixture. Cook over a low heat, stirring, until eggs are just set. Pile over toast.

25. Perfect jacket potatoes

Ingredients

50g light soft cheese

Squeeze lemon juice

1 hot-smoked salmon fillet
1 heaped tsp capers
A little lemon zét
1 baking
Potato oil

Method

Heat oven to 220C. Rub a little oil and seasoning over the potatoes, then bake on a baking sheet for 25 mins. Turn down the oven to 190 and bake for 1 hr-1 hr 15 mins more until the flesh is tender and the skin crisp and golden.

For a quicker option, prick a potato with a fork. Wrap in a sheet of kitchen paper and microwave on High for 8-10 mins until soft inside. For crisp skin, rub with a little oil, then flash under a hot grill, turning often. To serve, slice a cross in the centre, squeeze the base to 'pop' the top, then choose your favourite filling.

For the salmon and soft cheese filling, mix 50g light soft cheese with a squeeze lemon juice and seasoning. Pile into a jacket potato and flake 1 hot-smoked salmon fillet on top. Sprinkle with 1 heaped tsp capers and a little lemon zest.

26. Mexican turkey salad bowl

Ingredients

1 large flour tortilla

2 tbsp olive oil, Olive oil, Juice ½ lime

tbsp sliced jalapeños, plus 1 tbsp of vinegar from the jar handful crisp salad leaves

½ avocado, stoned & cut into chunks 1 tomato, chopped

½ small red onion, sliced
2 thick slices cooked turkey, shredded

1 tbsp cheddar, grated

Soured cream, to serve

Method

Heat oven to 220. To make a tortilla basket, soften the tortilla in the microwave for a few secs, then brush with a little of the oil and gently push the oiled side to line a small ovenproof bowl.

Line with foil and weigh with baking beans or a slightly smaller ovenproof bowl. Cook for 8-12 mins until crisp, allow to cool slightly before removing.

Make the dressing by mixing the oil, lime juice and vinegar, season. Mix the leaves, avocado, tomato, onion and turkey and toss with the dressing. Pile into the bowl and top with the cheese, jalapeños and a dollop of soured cream.

27. Mussels in red pesto

Ingredients

1 tsp olive oil

Olive oil

1 shallot, finely chopped

1 small glass white wine

Pinch crushed chilli flakes

500g clean live mussels

2 tbsp red pesto

Crusty bread, to serve

Method

Heat the oil in a large pan and cook the shallot for 4-5 mins until softened. Pour in the wine, add the chilli flakes and bubble for 2 mins.

Add the mussels. Cover and cook for 5 mins until all the shells have opened. Discard any that remain closed. Stir in the red pesto and toss well. Tip into a large bowl and serve with crusty bread.

28. Thai-style chicken and sweet potato

Ingredients

25g creamed coconut (from a block)

2 tsp soft brown sugar

1 tsp fish sauce

Fish sauce

2 tsp Thai green curry paste

½ sweet potato, peeled and cut into small cubes

1 small red pepper, deseeded and cut into small cubes

1 skinless chicken breast

Handful coriander leaves and a few lime wedges, to serve

Method

Heat oven to 200C. Dissolve the creamed coconut with 3 tbsp boiling water and mix to a smooth paste. Stir in the sugar, fish sauce and curry paste.

Place a large piece of baking parchment on a baking sheet. Arrange the sweet potato and pepper in the middle of the paper, clearing a space in the centre. Lay the chicken breast in the space and pour over the sauce. Fold over the top edges of the parchment to form a seal and scrunch up the ends like a sweet wrapper.

Cook in the oven for 25-30 mins or until the chicken is cooked through and the vegetables are tender. Sit the parcel on a dinner plate or shallow bowl and carefully open. Sprinkle with coriander and squeeze over some lime juice, to taste.

29. Salami and courgette flatbread

Ingredients

1 small courgette, thinly sliced

2 tsp olive oil

Pasta sauce

2 slices salami, cut into strips

25g emmental, grated

Method

Heat oven to 220C and place a griddle pan over a high heat. Toss the courgette slices in a bowl with the olive oil, oregano and seasoning. Lay the courgette slices on the griddle and cook for a few mins each side until just tender.

Place the flatbread on a baking sheet and spread with the pasta sauce. Arrange the courgette slices on top, before scattering over salami and cheese.

Place in the oven and bake for 8 mins until cheese has melted and the bread's edges are crisp.

30. Smart crab linguine

Ingredients

100 g linguine

1 tbsp olive oil

2 garlic cloves, finely sliced

2 tbsp low-fat cream fraîche

100g tub white crab mét ò 100g drained from a can handful roker, chopped, plus extra leaves to serve zest ½ lemon

1 tbsp toasted pine nuts

Method

Cook the linguine following pack instructions, reserving a little cooking liquid before you drain it.

Heat the olive oil in a frying pan. Add the garlic and cook gently to soften, but don't brown. Stir in the crème fraîche, crabmeat, chopped rocket and lemon zest, and gently heat through.

Tip in the cooked pasta and a little cooking liquid to help the sauce coat the pasta. Season and give everything a stir. Sprinkle with the pine nuts and remaining rocket leaves.

31. One-pot chicken pilaf

Ingredients

1 tsp sunflower oil

1 small onion, chopped

1 large or 2 small boneless, skinless chicken thigh fillets, cut into chunks

2 tsp curry paste (choose your favourite)

A third of a mug basmati rice

Ttwo-thirds of a mug chicken stock

1 mug frozen mixed vegetables

Half a mug frozen leaf spinach

Method

Heat the oil in a frying pan, then fry the onion for 5-6 mins until softened. Add the chicken pieces, fry for a further couple of mins just to colour the outside, then stir in curry paste and rice. Cook for another min.

Pour in the chicken stock and throw in any larger bits of frozen veg. Bring to the boil, lower the heat, then cover the pan with a lid. Cook for 10 mins, then stir in the remaining veg. Scatter over the spinach, cover, then cook for 10 mins more until all the stock is absorbed and the rice is tender. Give everything a good stir, season to taste, then tuck in.

32. Chicken soba noodles

Ingredients

85g bundle soba or buckwheat noodles

Drizzle of sesame oil

8 mangetout

Mangettout with papaya & bean sprouts on a white plate

1 small carrot

½ red chilli

1 tbsp toasted sesame seeds

Handful shredded cooked chicken

Soy sauce

Method

Cook the noodles, drain well, then toss with a drizzle sesame oil.

Finely slice the mangetout, cut the carrot into matchsticks and deseed and slice the red chilli.

Add to the noodles with the toasted sesame seeds and some shredded cooked chicken, if you have it. Pack with a small portion of soy sauce.

33. Steak, chips and pepper sauce

Ingredients

2 tbsp olive oil

1 large potato, cut into chunky chips, skin left on

1 fillet steak

1 tbsp red wine vinegar

125ml beef stock

2 heaped tbsp extra thick double cream

Method

Heat oven to 200C. Put 1 tbsp oil in a small roasting tin and heat up in the oven. Boil the potatoes in salted water for 3 mins before draining and letting steam-dry for a few mins. Season, carefully toss in the hot oil and cook for 30-35 mins until crisp and golden.

When the chips are nearly done, heat the rest of the oil in a frying pan. Season the steak with lots of freshly ground pepper and a little salt, then fry for 2-3 mins on each side, depending on how rare you like it. Rest for 5 mins while you make the sauce.

Pour excess oil from the pan and add the vinegar. Bubble, then add the stock and boil until reduced by half. Stir through the cream, bubbling to thicken a little, then add as much extra pepper as you like. Serve with steak, chips and peas.

34. Shepherd's pie potatoes

Ingredients

2 tsp butter

½ onion, chopped

140g lean minced

Beef 250ml beef stock

1 tsp Worcestershire sauce

1 tbsp tomato purée

1 large jacket potato, baked

Small handful grated cheddar

Method

Heat oven to 200C. Melt half the butter in a non-stick pan. Cook the onion for 3-4 mins, then increase the heat and add the mince. Fry for a further 3-4 mins until the beef has browned. Stir in the stock, Worcestershire sauce, tomato purée and some seasoning. Gently bubble for 15-20 mins until the mince is tender and the sauce has thickened.

To assemble, cut the jacket potato in half lengthways and scoop the flesh into a small bowl, leaving the skin intact. Mash the potato with the remaining butter and season well. Divide the mince between the potato skins, then cover with the mash. Transfer the potatoes to a baking dish, sprinkle with cheese, then bake for 15-20 mins until golden. Serve with your favourite veg.

35. Oven baked swai

Ingredients

2 (4 ounce) fillets swai fish

Salt and ground black pepper to taste

1 tablespoon olive oil, or as needed

1 onion, chopped

1 clove garlic, minced

1 (14.5 ounce) can petite diced tomatoes

Directions

Preheat oven to 200C. Place the swai fish in a glass casserole dish and season with salt and black pepper.

Heat olive oil in a large skillet over medium heat; cook and stir onion until softened, about 10 minutes. Add garlic and cook until fragrant, about 1 minute. Pour tomatoes over onion mixture; cook and stir until heated through, about 5 minutes. Spoon tomato mixture over fish.

Bake in the preheated oven until fish flakes easily with a fork, about 20 minutes.

36. Black bean breakfast bowl

Ingredients

2 tablespoons olive oil

4 eggs, beaten

1 (15 ounce) can black beans, drained and rinsed

1 avocado, peeled and sliced

1/4 cup salsa

Salt and ground black pepper to taste

Directions

Heat olive oil in a small pan over medium heat. Cook and stir eggs until eggs are set, 3 to 5 minutes.

Place black beans in a microwave-safe bowl. Heat on High in the microwave until warm, about 1 minute.

Divide warmed black beans between two bowls.

Top each bowl with scrambled eggs, avocado, and salsa. Season with salt and black pepper.

37. Egg curry
Ingredients

2 tablespoons vegetable oil, 1 onion, sliced

1 teaspoon garlic paste

1/2 teaspoon ginger paste

1 tablespoon ground coriander

1 teaspoon ground cumin

1/2 teaspoon ground turmeric

1/2 teaspoon chile powder

1/4 teaspoon ground black pepper

1/4 cup tomato puree

1 1/4 cups water

1 tablespoon vinegar, Salt to taste

4 hard-boiled eggs, halved

Directions

Heat oil in a large pot over medium heat. Add onion; cook and stir until browned, about 5 minutes. Stir in garlic and ginger paste. Mix in coriander, cumin, turmeric, chile powder, and black pepper; cook until fragrant, about 1 minute. Add tomato puree; cook until curry thickens, about 4 minutes.

Pour water into the pot; bring sauce to a boil. Stir in vinegar and salt. Slip eggs into the pot; cook until flavors combine, about 5 minutes.

38. Baby spinach omelet

Ingredients

2 eggs

1 cup torn baby spinach leaves

1 1/2 tablespoons grated Parmesan cheese

1/4 teaspoon onion powder

1/8 teaspoon ground nutmeg

Salt and pepper to taste

Directions

In a bowl, beat the eggs, and stir in the baby spinach and Parmesan cheese. Season with onion powder, nutmeg, salt, and pepper.

In a small skillet coated with cooking spray over medium heat, cook the egg mixture about 3 minutes, until partially set. Flip with a spatula, and continue cooking 2 to 3 minutes. Reduce heat to low, and continue cooking 2 to 3 minutes, or to desired doneness.

39. Skillet salmon with tomato quinoa
Ingredients

2 teaspoons canola oil

3 cloves garlic, finely chopped

1 cup cooked quinoa

3/4 cup canned diced tomatoes

1/4 teaspoon paprika, salt, pepper

1 cup loosely packed baby spinach

2 tablespoons fresh basil, chopped

1 salmon filet (3 ounces, skin removed)

Directions

Heat oven to 425°.

In a small ovenproof skillet over medium heat, heat oil. Add garlic and cook, stirring, until fragrant, about 1 minute. Add quinoa, tomatoes, and paprika. Season with salt and pepper. Cook, stirring, until heated through. Add spinach and basil and stir to wilt.

Season salmon liberally with salt and pepper. Place salmon on top of quinoa mixture. Transfer to oven and roast 8 to 12 minutes (the thicker your fillets, the longer it will take) for medium rare, 12 to 18 minutes for well done.

Let leftovers cool completely before storing in an airtight container in the fridge.

40. Stir-fried chicken with corn and millet

Ingredients

3 ounces boneless, skinless chicken thighs, cut into 1-inch pieces

Salt

Pepper

½ tablespoon olive oil

2 cloves garlic, sliced thin

½ cup fresh corn kernels (from 1 small ear)

2/3 cup cooked millet

2 tablespoons fresh parsley,chopped

¼ lime, juiced

1/4 medium-size ripe avocado, chopped into 1/2-inch pieces

Directions

Season chicken on all sides with salt and pepper. In a large skillet over medium heat, heat olive oil. Add chicken and garlic and cook, stirring occasionally, until chicken is cooked through, about 4 minutes.

Add corn and cook, stirring, just until it starts to soften, about 2 minutes more.

Add millet, parsley, and juice. Cook, stirring, until heated through. Top with avocado.

41. Shrimp Scampi For One
Ingredients

1/4 pound 21 count shrimp, about 6

1 large shallot, minced

2-3 cloves garlic, minced

2 Tablespoons butter

3 Tablespoons cream

Splash of white wine (optional)

1/8 Teaspoon crushed red pepper flakes (optional)

Parmesan cheese (optional)

Salt and pepper

Spaghetti

1/4 Cup reserved pasta water

Directions

Cook the pasta according to package. Reserve some of the cooking water for the sauce later. Drain the pasta and set it aside.

Mince garlic and shallots and clean the shrimp if they aren't already cleaned.

Add butter to pot over medium heat. Once hot and melted, add the cleaned shrimp and cook for 90 seconds per side. Then add shallots and garlic and cook for another 30 seconds until soft.

Add a splash of white wine, and the crushed red pepper. Try not to overcook them.

Add cream to the shrimp and stir. The sauce should reduce nicely.

Add pasta back into the pot and stir to combine. Season with salt and pepper. If sauce is too thick, add a bit of reserved pasta water to thin it out. Don't make it too thin though!

42. Healthy Pita Pizza with Goat Cheese

Ingredients

4 whole wheat pitas, 1 small red onion

Handful thyme sprigs

1 pound tomatoes (heirloom or multi-colored, if desired)

2 cups shredded mozzarella cheese

4 ounces goat cheese, Salt

Fresh ground pepper, Olive oil (optional)

Instructions

Place a pizza stone in the oven and preheat to 450°F.

Place pita directly on the oven grate and pre-bake 3 minutes per side, then flip and bake another 3 minutes.

Thinly slice the red onion. Roughly chop the thyme. Using a serrated knife, thinly slice the tomatoes.

When the pitas are crisp, remove them from the oven. The top each with 1/2 cup mozzarella, then tomatoes, onions, and thyme leaves. Add dollops of goat cheese. Sprinkle liberally with kosher salt, especially the tomatoes. If desired, drizzle with olive oil.

Bake until the cheese is melted, about 5 minutes. Remove from the oven, cut into wedges, and serve.

43. Chanterelle Omelet with Fines Herbes
Ingredients

1 large egg, beaten until smooth with a tablespoon water

1 Tbsp Creme fraiche or sour cream

1 tsp chopped fresh fines herbes- (Equal parts: Tarragon, Parsley, Chives, Chervil-slice the chives individually, chop the other herbs together, then mix all when finished)

1.5 ounces fresh chanterelles, preferably in small buttons (a generous handful if you don't have a digital scale)

Salt and pepper to taste

1 tbsp grapeseed oil, or other searing oil like vegetable, or canola

1 tbsp unsalted butter

Fresh greens and flowers, optional, dressed lightly with lemon, olive oil, and a pinch of salt

Method

If the chanterelles are dirty, brush them, then swish in cold water quickly, and dry on a towel.

Very clean chanterelles may simply be brushed without washing.

Whisk the eggs, chopped herbs, and sour cream or crème fraiche.

Heat the oil in a small cast iron skillet or a small teflon pan. (I used a small six inch cast iron with 2 inch sides). When the oil is hot and just begins to smoke, add the drained and completely dry chanterelles to the pan, cooking in the oil until they are lightly caramelized and golden, about 2-3 minutes.

Season the chanterelles to taste with salt and pepper, then add the butter and melt.

Add the egg mixture to the pan, let this cook for 30 seconds, stirring occasionally to form soft curds which should only lightly envelop the chanterelles, keeping them visible and not hidden under egg.

When the egg mixture begins to coagulate, then turn the heat off of the pan and allow the eggs to set with the residual heat of the pan.

Finish the omelet by seasoning with a touch of fine salt like kosher or flaked salt and serve immediately, topped with the fresh greens if using.

44. 1-minute coffee cake in a mug

Ingredients

Cake

2 tablespoons of sugar (I like to use brown, I have also tried it with Truvia, which works well)

1 tablespoon of butter

2 tablespoons of Greek yogurt

Dash of vanilla

1/4 teaspoon of cinnamon

Dash of nutmeg

1/4 cup all-purpose flour

1/8 teaspoon of baking powder, Pinch of salt

Topping

1 tablespoon of butter (use cold butter straight from the fridge for the crumbliest topping)

2 tablespoons of flour

1 tablespoons of brown sugar

1/4 teaspoon of cinnamon, Dash of nutmeg

Instructions

Place the butter in a mug. Microwave for 10-15 seconds to soften the butter. Remove from the microwave and stir in all ingredients, except for the flour. Mix until well-combined. Fold the flour in, making sure to not over-mix. Using your spoon gently push the batter together into the bottom of the mug. Set aside.

To make the topping, use your fingers to mix the butter, flour, sugar and spices together to form a crumbly mixture. Add to the top of the cake.

Microwave the cake for 60 seconds (the time may vary depending on your microwave, but it should take anywhere from 50-90 seconds). Serve immediately with milk or coffee.

45. Single-serving microwave brownie

Ingredients

2 tbsp (10g) unsweetened cocoa powder (measured correctly)

1 ½ tbsp (11g) whole wheat flour (measured correctly)

2 tbsp (30 ml) water

1 tbsp (15g) plain nonfat Greek yogurt

2 tsp agave

⅛ tsp vanilla extract

Instructions

Lightly coat a 1-cup ramekin with nonstick cooking spray. Set aside.

In a small bowl, whisk together the cocoa and flour. In a separate bowl, stir together the water, yogurt, agave, and vanilla. Add the dry ingredients into the wet, stirring just until incorporated.

Pour the batter into the prepared ramekin, gently shaking back and forth until the top is smooth. Microwave at 40% POWER for 2 minutes and 15 seconds (2:15). Let the brownie sit for at least 3 minutes before eating.

46. Chicken bruschetta pasta salad

Ingredients

1/2 cup boiled pasta, drained (60g dry weight)

1/2 red onion, finely chopped

1 tomato, finely chopped

Fresh basil leaves, finely chopped

1 small chicken breast, (135g), pre-grilled and seasoned with (or any garlic powder or seasoning of choice)

1 teaspoon garlic olive oil

Drizzle of balsamic glaze

Instructions

Simply mix pasta, onion and tomatoes together in a bowl

Mix through the oil and season with a little salt (to suit your tastes)

Top with chicken and drizzle with balsamic glaze

Sprinkle with some parmesan cheese. Enjoy!

47. Mediterranean grilled cheese sandwich

Ingredients

2 slices bread

1-2 tsp butter

2 slices feta cheese

1/4 cup kale

3 red onion slices

1 slice tomato

2 tbsp California black ripe olives

Instructions

Butter one side of each piece of bread, then place one of them butter-side down into a skillet.

Add the cheese, kale, onions, tomato, and olives on top of the bread, then place the second piece butter-side up on top.

Grill sandwich on the one side before carefully flipping over and grilling on the other side until cheese has melted.

48. Sweet potato breakfast skillet for one

Ingredients

1/2 cup chopped sweet potato

1/3-1/2 cup cooked chicken breast, chopped

1 egg

1/2 small avocado

Pinch of salt and pepper

2 tsp extra virgin olive oil

Instructions

Preheat the oven to 350 degrees.

Preheat a small cast iron skillet over medium-heat. Once skillet is hot, add the oil and the sweet potato. Season with a small pinch of salt and pepper and stir occasionally until sweet potato is cooked through. This should take about 5-7 minutes, depending on how small you chopped them.

When potato is cooked through, add the chicken and saute for another 1-2 minutes, just to warm the chicken all the way through.

Move the potato mixture around to make a hole in the center of the skillet. Carefully crack the egg and drop it into the hole. Sprinkle the egg with a tiny bit of salt and pepper.

Carefully transfer the skillet to the oven and bake for about 5 minutes for a runny yolk. If you want the yolk to be harder, bake for 7-8 minutes.

Remove from the oven and garnish with sliced avocado. You can eat it straight from the skillet, just be careful to not burn yourself and always set the skillet on top of a towel or hot plate. If you are worried, then transfer all of it to a plate, and enjoy!

Courgette

49. Zucchini noodles with garlic and oil

Ingredients

12 ounces zucchini, 2-3 small

2 Teaspoons olive oil

1 small clove of garlic, minced

1/4 Teaspoon red pepper flakes

1/2 Teaspoon ground sea salt

1/2 Teaspoon freshly ground black pepper

Optional:

Freshly grated parmesan cheese

1–2 eggs – cooked over-easy, or however you like them

Instructions

Wash the zucchini and slice off both ends creating a nice, flat surface.

Spiralize the zucchini, or use a julienne peeler to create veggie noodles.

Preheat a 9″ cast iron pan over medium-high heat.

While the pan is heating, assemble and prepare your other ingredients.

Add the olive oil to the hot pan, followed by the garlic, red pepper flakes, sea salt, and black pepper. Sauté just until fragrant but not brown – about 30 seconds.

Add the zucchini noodles to the pan and sauté until just tender, 3-5 minutes.

Serve the zucchini noodles immediately topped with your choice of toppings.

50. Mexican stuffed sweet potato

Ingredients

1 large sweet potato pierced with a fork several times, and wrapped tightly in foil.

Cashew cheese crumbles:

1/4 cup cashews

1/4 teaspoon extra virgin olive oil

1 teaspoon lemon juice

Sea salt and ground black pepper to taste

Filling:

1/2 teaspoon avocado oil

1/3 cup frozen corn kernels thawed

1/2 cup cooked black beans

1 cup chopped fresh spinach

1/4 cup chopped cilantro

1/4 teaspoon chipotle chili powder

1/4 teaspoon paprika

1/4 teaspoon cumin

Sea salt and pepper to taste

Juice from one lime

Salsa optional

Instructions

Preheat the oven to 385° Bake the sweet potato for 1 hour until soft to the touch when pinched. Remove and set aside. Leave the foil on. In a small food processor process the ingredients for the cashew cheese crumbles until the mixture looks like pebbles.

For the filling; heat an iron skillet on medium high heat. Add the avocado oil and spread evenly on the surface of the pan. Add the corn and toss in the pan until it begins to brown. Turn down the heat to medium and add the beans and spices. Toss to coat and cook for three minutes. Add the spinach and cilantro and cook until just wilted. Remove the pan from the heat

Take the foil off of the potato and put on a plate. Slice down the middle and separate. Fill with the corn and bean mixture and top with the cashew cheese crumbles and salsa. Sprinkle with some fresh cilantro if desired.

MENU